W0081476

WRONG WINDS

AHMAD ALMALLAH

Fonograf Editions
Portland, OR

Copyright © 2025 • Ahmad Almallah • All rights reserved
Cover and text design by Mike Corrao

Cover art: *Flying Lesson #07 (detail)*, 2010 by Hani Zurob

First Edition, Second Printing

FONO36

Published by Fonograf Editions
www.fonografeditions.com

For information about permission to reuse any material
from this book, please contact Fonograf Ed. at info@
fonografeditions.com.

Distributed by NYU Press
NYUPress.org

[clmp]

Fonograf Editions is a proud member of the Community of
Literary Magazines and Presses

ISBN: 978-1-964499-48-2
ISBN (ebook): 978-1-964499-50-5
ISBN (library ed. hardcover): 978-1-964499-49-9
LCCN: 2024947030

WRONG WINDS

FONOGRAF EDITIONS

CONTENTS

Carry hate
In front of you and harmony behind.

— Gwendolyn Brooks

for Gaza…
for weathering all the wrong winds

AFTER Al-SHANFARA

ولكنّ نفسا مُرَّة لا تُقيمُ بي   على الذام إلا ريثما أتحوّلُ

◆

الشّنفرى

◆

but this proud bitter self
has no place in it
for injury;
it scorns
till eyes turn
toward an
other
beyond those places
in the past I'll leave—
setting out in me.

1

LOOSE STRINGS

What does it mean to be a poet, another "Homer"
going home? Trying to find one?

      Is it time to prepare?

             Here:

another trip to that place, that first encounter
with air—

From the river I look to see and imagine
the dark waters of that sea, where
I've never been. Closed to me, the birth
place of my mother, Jaffa, Yazour…
Strange facts hang in the vision like loose
stings, and because we're helpless, we
have to label everything and live with

     the fallacies of naming:

        and so

        sigh after sigh, I sigh:

تذكرت أمي والليالي الخواليا —

فما الصمت إلا صمتك الآن في الدجى
وطيف خيال منك لم يأت جازيا

فأصبحت أذكي نار يومي بعبرتي
فما الشوق محمودا ولا الوجد شافيا

BEFORE GAZA, A FALL

The sick leaves hang—
      on tight.

There are not enough—
      numbers
      to
occupy the count?

Death does its work.

      Disappears.

      And the sick
          turn to
      the ground.

Then the river hits,

makes way.

Don't repeat.

      Repeat:

Pollen and dirt
to the side. What holds
the future? A nothing
is not enough. Gaza,
        had to
        go in numbers.
And now *you*, who are
you?   And
that sum:
        where now
lasts beyond
                Never.

        ♦

At the construction site.

Memory and flowers.

Metal and wood.

Some things fall too hard.
Traffic above water holds
the scene.

To   gather:

Eyes think shots. Boom.
        Bullets.

Did we have to predict the
        Future?

Birds drenched in filth—
        This is how
        the world

        works
            breaks:

And the moon: a half
        egg-shell
        in the sky.

A NOTE ON DISASTER

for Huda Fakhreddine

How will you write disaster in when this line is
over? What will you do to prevent it from being
the end? How do you seek it in and out?
For a long while I could not jot it down: Language.
I kept writing it off in an Arabic, that I called mine,
breaking under the weight of year after years
of what I did not know what to call: Distance.
When I met you, I did not know how long it would be
before I discovered the source of the sound. It
was already broken and I was always stepping on
the pieces. You helped me put something with
the other. I never thanked you for it. I was broken,
until you reminded me that the hand is only made
to handle, and even so at times it cannot. Disaster
is stronger. Disaster, dear Huda, is always at hand.

A HOLY LAND, WASTED

with Huda Fakhreddine

1

April is not that bad actually:
August is the cruelest month! It may be…
But say what you may of memory and desire,
the faint smell of semen
trees, the Americans brought
to the "Middle East"—those
strange words we inhaled in
the garden of Bethlehem Uni,
the same smell at AUB, another
American campus on native lands.
We looked at one another,
and we couldn't put words
to work, we thought of the naked
figures we wounded our bodies into—
all for what?!
                    Marie Marie
is my Deutsch instructor, the one
who wiped chalk on her butt cheeks,
only to add insult to injury. Of course:
we were horny teenagers waiting
for a sign of the flesh to make
itself visible. Did you know,
dear reader, that we learned German
in Palestine? What a strange

destiny it was to be sent to the
German Headmaster's office
when I dealt my English teacher
a verbal blow. He asked me
"upon mischief": would you
drop yourself in a well if some-
one told you to. I said: it really depends,
dear master,

          on the depth of the well,
          of course!

Table meets chair: I tell you, there is no need
to make grand statements
that have been all made
in the past, anyway…there are chairs, and
tables—everywhere:
some of them squeak when dragged, some
doze off all day, not knowing what has been
sitting on them—but the tables don't care
much for anything, they see what the
chairs go through, they see in the Hofgarten –
how they are left feet up all night:
it's a disaster recurring with some regularity now:
since the creation of tables and chairs,
and although the two have lived together
for some time, both maintain they have
nothing to do with one another—too completely,
different species of things, sharing some
physical ground, but lacking
chemistry.

Table meets chair: the game of chess
remains the most played board
game in the world. How could
this be in the age of jolts and flashes?
Where do they find the time
to arrange tragedy on the board,
plot and strategy?
Where do they find pawns
to sacrifice themselves, one square
at a time, to accept the smaller fates,
while kings and queens huddle
backstage, twirling their fingers,
expecting glory to meet them halfway?

Table meets chair: In an age of boredom, they map
their courses to glory from a distance.
They scheme, from a distance,
when there is only one recourse:
Touch, skin on skin, more or less,
        a body to offer:
        one's own as proof
        or someone else's as loot.

The river has its tents. Apparently.
And because we are, dear Pal, the people
of the tents—not because
of our Bedouin pasts, and all that
poetry, just because we at every bend
are killed, our blood
spilled.

Against the rivers
and their beds, East
and West banks, we mine
the land with nothing
but our feet.

Let's stop there. No need to repeat
the old record, broken.
Please turn the volume up.
Hear the screams:
It's scratching again.
Safiyya, could you please bring
the volume down?! Hand me
my down pills or will you
hang me instead?
I can't face the world.
Let's stay in, and drink
our blood soup! Oh but the hours
are coming into play: kill kill
kill the hours. It's not good

for your nerves to watch
all that news, the sights
of dead children: not good
for your sleep. Please, Safiyya. Shut
down your screens. But beware
and listen carefully. Do nothing.
Do not shoot yourself
in the foot. And those shadows we
see on screen: how could
they go up against the tanks with
no shoes? Barbaric! Their
killings are not timed
well, not timely.
It's impossible to watch it
all.

Safiyya, Safiyya, I'm going
to sleep. I'll take you with me
one day, and you'll see. For now
I want you to focus on your
teeth. Look at yourself in the
mirror. Hold on tight.
Do you see a face beside
yours? Look no more if you
do! Yes. Good night, Safiyya,
good night, dear shadows in the
background. Good night, dear
dead babies. Now you'll finally
be able to sleep, and give us all
a moment's peace.

Son of man, a heap of broken
images, you say, and I say, then
she says and he says. What do
we know of the big heap? STDs
sound awfully abbreviated, and
the kids do get their feed every
dark day. Clickety clack, clickety
clack: no one knows root or
                    branch:
                    Yes, the
                    sun is
          warming over our heads, or
is it the earth getting unbearably
hot? The moats boil beyond our siege;
to motes the world crumbles, shattered
like these useless *mots*. What's this
talk of French stuff, and warm
kisses that are two centuries old?
Well, cool it down, Bro.
Buy yourself another century.
Be done with it you dusty fool!
This is the apocalypse in you talking.
This is the time of beginnings,
of ends. Who really cares? Well,
I do. I really do, and I promise
you, whoever you are, another
wasted land, in another promised
land, another time and another

dimension, where the same folk
will rule again, and bury us all
in their gardens, over and over, in
this, the first life
and the other.

Tomorrow or the day after, I'll
pack my things and off to hell.
Another visit to Palestine.
I tell you,
I have a fucked-up land, and
a fucked-up family in that neck
of the woods, as the Americans
would have it: all in ashes, all
in ash. I tell you, my tongue
is tied up today, and maybe will
forever be after this and that
genocide. I tell you straight out, but you,
you want me to suffer my pronouncements
and syllables.

The best way to solve
your problem is to save time:
                eradicate me.
I just don't seem to add up
to more than a zero on the side
of numerical figures that only
appear to you, when your work is done.

Phlebas was really the Palestinian.
Phoenician was just the story he told
to pass under the wire,
slip through the edges of cities,
        unreal.
    He counted his bones every night,
his teeth too, thinking of rubble. He dreamt of the cry of gulls,
and the deep sea swell and wished for death by water,
a rendezvous with the sea, at least,
an escape from the siege
of burning sands, at last.
    He passed the stages of his age and youth,
waiting for the rocket to fall. No death,
the sound of death only.
    Gentile or Jew, O you
who click and swipe, turn and fold
the blood drenched screens into your eyes,
consider Phlebas, who was once handsome and tall as you.
    He didn't drown. Thirsty, his body overflowed
with unlived days. They spilled out,
      and a flood of blood,
          trickled in the sand.

At the checkpoint it's better to keep the
         page
blank: owner—unknown, and
in case of losing or loss, please
keep the blanks as a souvenir. This is
the holy land, where tourists come and go
thinking of Michael Angelo…oh how lovely
it is to imagine the plight and toil of others, when
you don't have to deliver anything to anyone!

Let me rephrase, numbers are all, and what did the "I" learn
from exile? That putting a numerical figure on loss
is all numbers! What if the figure turns odd, that's just
how luck goes, isn't that right? Here is there, and
there is here…we've learned that from desire: how
to own and impress on others numbers numbers numbers.
      Yeah, good
is bad, and bad is good, and a certain command
of your narrative
is necessary to keep at it—i.e.
the more the merrier, i.e. once more: in what's recommended
in modernist writing practices, that's also to say: I have to
      tell you
the details…but what if memory fails
and files all the wrong winds in your brain, so even
when you face the details, you have no place to file
them…in the self? In the mind? And as the recommendations
pile up in front of your facts: 23 years of absence

mean that you've been present somewhere, which
        means...
that all the loss involved in claiming the numerical figure
"as a fact of life" can't be captured—time flies on the wrong
wings now, where all memories end up, or down,
irrelevant: a burden that can only be carried by the body
of a person carrying all the numbers impressed upon a
        personal history,
creating
an invisible label that no amount of identity
can convey.

MY TONGUE IS TIED UP TODAY

&
So my tongue is tied up today,
maybe I am certain it will
be, something between
                    jaws.

        Maybe it could be
        just that slab of meat
        on its own

without any language:
and then I'll swallow
my pride without the
            bitter   taste
                        of meaning
                                    and

            then
my mother, my mother land
and   Tongue
will call onto me my name.

&
Something against
        those leaves
in this country that
        sides
                against me every
                time, bombs
                fall on Palestine!

It's fall. The fall!
The one leaf that follows me I fail
to catch

before hitting ground—
Why did I buy this lie?
Or, why
        can't I buy it?

The blowers blow
leaves and dust
        in the face of—
        words
        falling
        again: why…
        why
can't I catch any
        of them?

&

For my eyes, this is…
forget it! How many
times have we said
it. If we'd be true to
any cause, we would
simply stop, because
no name, can or could—
no, yes-no-amount of
longing can take back
what we've applied to
our sufferings in
                    numbers.

&
The snow that serves
          as a smudge,
thalj is another
key—the door is
locked like metaphor:
none know the secret
to any.

          We walk among the
          flags, covering the
          ground with the
          deaths of another
                    land—

Yes: this is the cold setting
in—this is the nothing that
          there was.

&

Winter is the outcome:
something of the Fall
remains in those names
hung for the eyes to
come to turn and terms
        of disaster—
Name the nameless now!
Where is my hand—some
find theirs where they left them
some look for fingers
among the rubble:
        and some live
        to see others,
die.

&
We keep repeating the count:
texts, messages, more messages
and texts…till meaning is
just in a loop:
repeating itself to
         itself.

WRONG WINDS

for Paul Celan

0

In Berlin there is the sadness
of old murder.

In Granada there was the sadness
of murdered names:

names

        unable to make up their minds
        about origins.

Silence doesn't come easy in
        Spain.
One has to wait
        like the wind

for the moment to transform itself
into a scream

and silence might then appear
        for a second:

        a headless statue
        without a name.

Mirror: [O, I look in this sheltered
        glass
for the figures beside
the image: what do I
lack? Only that connection
to your courage
            not to endure life
            when, for you,
    there
        was no more]

I, you, and the others like
to generalize:
To console myself I say —
I belong to my head. No:
I won't ask Gods to pray
for us like you did. No,
und nein, just like nine
months of murder can't
cancel a new-born wind
in those wombs that
have failed to carry the
fractions of your numbered
past, among the ones who
placed a body in your every
thought, and fanned the
wrong
winds—
the ones coming to
you in no guises, in no act of the
breeze—Schief mit what, what will
make you shed
blood without
any tears?

Mirror: [Berlin knows its
dead. Without design, I'm
lost. Once more. Did I mention
"without design"? Because without

it, I stumble on your Sundays, Berlin, O
without design: I'm where the living tend
to their dead: "Pflanzenabfälle."
What does it mean to be a found object, in place
of the dead, not dying?
Because for many, this found cemetery
is only a path, for most
a shortcut. That way. Yes.
This way. Nein. Like a new-
born wind
          we
know the dead more
than we think]

2

You, who inhaled the fumes
of German syllables, because
that clunky thing gave you
chance and words to pin against
the body that you suffered silently
because, again, you wanted to give
        w   ords, a   wink:
        a bleeding form that
        cannot be divided by
              teeth.

But there is no such thing
as belonging without edges.

Say it!

"I belong to kill my other!"

Berlin knows these words
because it's not a city—it's
sour and sudden like
 a cherry
        inside a piece of
             burnt bread.

Mirror: [The kids find their sticks, and if you eye
one of them, they'll all eye you back, and raise their sticks

against you. This is no surprise.
The stick is the original weapon, and Hugo, the name of
    that little
shit, when called by his father, drops his weapon
to save his name]

3

So tell me, whoever
     art thou:
Can I swallow the scene
instead of framing it?

Mirror: [Berlin in this summer green hides
her dead again. On Sundays the park fills with feet,
and hatred is a thing
nurtured in the news. There is death,
coming from every
where—let's not name names
lest we
are

     accused of
     forgetfulness]

4

Poisoned by your name, you
declared that our bodies are
only feet, dug in the dirt. If
we lack movement, we are
                    chained. Didn't
al-Mutanabbi make it before us
to such reductions. Didn't
his doctor reduce his tied-up
soul to some ailment unworthy
of poets? What malady could
come from food or drink?! You,
on the other hand, suffered in
concentration the maladies of
hunger. Your body was that of
others: feet dug into the ground
till there was no body attached:
were you not like all the others
named, the victor's victim?

Mirror: [After so many mornings
                    in this place or
with it: Arabic comes from
        a passer-by,
ears perk up
        to pick up sound.
Then eyes witness
        the face that said.

Why can't the eye shut I?

And because I eye the lie that's me,
something about our inherit Arab-ness,
another line by al-Mutanabbi that says,

> Love less O heart, love less,
> I see you giving love to one, underserving.

Words overwhelm, and say
      STOP.
We, like the body
      can carry
      no more]

5

What's the heart of a place? Is it a pond? Is it
a wound? Is it the puddles made by rain? What's
all this wounded beauty?

    A black cat passes like a cloud. It scares but does not
scratch. There is fear. There might be more to fear,
because here in Berlin
the possible outnumbers the impossible, and you have to
    guard yourself
from all that is available.

    Then my new-found friend in some bar tells me: take a line
    of cocaine!
Put down your pen!

Mirror: [On the wall: a bottle and a poet, and if I describe
    things as they are
I'm sure to lose something of the truth.

    The language that binds us to ourselves is not there, not
here either: Is that what a poet is supposed to find,
among the heap of ruins
    and waste—
a city, like you, like others in Europe?

And in the distance, "We,"
the poets?   We
clasp onto meaning
as though life depends on it, and then
we clasp some more, without much
thinking or thought, and in our minds

      we are always right,
and never:

      could I ever
be
a bottle
carrying a message

      —not a poet]

Behind bars we are all
striped. The animal in us can't
hide for long. We lock the door
to create our prison. We turn the key
to prevent bodies from reaching our own: can
we imagine what's out there if we don't draw
what bounds us? Eyes try to notice and record:
You can see more clearly if you are blind: yes—
Just as much. There are walkers and talkers,
laughter and laughers. Just as much.
There are fathers
and fuckers—   and the blue ball—
           that's not the world
           rolls down the street
           beyond school bounds.

Mirror: [The rest of the story might be as dark as those
     German clouds
in May or June…or July? Above Berlin, there is Germany,
above Germany, there is Europe, above all, there is
the
sky. What else did you think?
         I hide in front of signs. This is my usual trick.
         I want to be something like they are—
And the green of the streets and parks hides in plain sight.
How can summer be in a place
that knows so much ash]

Places don't make sense to me or you. We are
here and there, only because the body is
      a vehicle.
And now after the flood
      of images, and emojis, we
don't need any mirror
      to look at ourselves.
      We already know
 the truth.
                Now, what will it
                do to us?

Mirror: [Broken
or not, this is all unreal, surreal,
so real! Word by word, I put my pen
to play, only to reduce this
place to what it is, and whoever tells
me, your words are a matter of…
      Let's not go there.
      Let's get out of here.
      Mince your words.

I say, to myself,
      as I always do:
      I want to forget you.

 You,
 City of Fumes: why can't you sit straight with yourself—

Dark matter evades all matter, because it's the abuse
of color, in some way or another...I see the crowds coming
    to fill
their cups with your darkness. How is it that so many murders
could produce this wiped-out vanity. Europe flatters
itself with your destiny and diversity,

        and all that beauty
        that can't be put together.]

SOME VERSES FOR THE DERPRESSED REBEL

for Federico García Lorca

1

♦

Fame is a B. You received its
fatal sting—Lorca: your house
is there, where it used to be.
They made a park around it
in your name.

It's some summer. El sol
es el major torero: memory,
remains and ruins in your
name I hear.   Then birds
fill the sky like ash in this
summer heat. Unbearable!
Just like the statues they planted
          in your figure.

When poets become others'
ornaments…what do you think?
Is it possible to save you from
yourself now, or are you
          forever?

The ports of your country, have
traded in gold and blood, and
much unwanted foreignness—
Or is it foreign-hood?—that is
Here. Did these Moorish states
of the mind...make you
who you are? You gave your
body, in unsatisfied desire,
            to that faraway place
            where the ruins spoke
            to poets, and reminded
you of who you are.

In your garden, a lemon tree
collets dust, as it should do—
Its fruit is dried up from heat.
This is the city of the farness
you nurtured like a seed. This
ornament of a city, Granada:
another fruit? There might be
no names, familiar to you now.
Some things are better off
unnamed? I can't help but
reason with your ashes. Names
become the first steppings
            into ruin, yes?
Name a thing, and you've
marked it for the end, of
imagination? And unless you
are willing to accept your

names misspelled back to
you, then don't name a
thing. Keep it floating in
anonymous darkness, then
weave the bees, stitch them
          to their honey.
They won't sting you that way, and out
of their buzzing, maybe a song
          will follow.

◆

Only so:　　　I keep yesterdays—
I fill my pockets with scraps
and scribbles.

Yesterdays
beckon a reduction of every
thing, to one crime:
are we talking
genocide now?

Who calls what and where?
Recollection is A. going mad
about how to reduce, and de-
duct, then add up, and fret
over the whole, that wants
to part with all other parts.

Listen now!
Granada is your birth-
fact. We've established
the only place. No need
to name names again: I go
looking for translations,
for edging the meanings
that exist beside sounds.
I believe they assassinate

that in your translation
to tongues that are stuck
in languages. You are a
rebel. Reduced to a poet.
A martyr, dressed up like
an Arab, and maybe trying
to fuck like one, but surely—
trying to get fucked like one.
I see: the flesh attracted you to
poetry. The forms made
fun of your facts, and
then a conclusion has
been drawn about your
               deaths:

He was a "man,"
a martyr for what defiles
manhood. He wanted
to recreate the blade
and the rifle as the new
tools for poetry. He shot
in the dark often. No one
dropped dead. But he did
kill the echo. His slicing
of the wind destroyed
his vision. Perspective was
of no use to him. He slept.
He dreamt, and slept
some more and dreamt—
and he managed to receive,

at the same time, between
one moment of wakefulness
and the other, every injury
that was dealt to him.

WOOK

When the world ends
—as in the now—we'll
have to turn books to
their source, and use
them as burning wood.

For now: I look at my
stack—of scrap books?
Mostly wood on wood
doesn't burn on its own.
What will I part with
first to keep warm, or

cook my self something?
Because you can't eat a
book, not for sustenance
anyway! Or could I make
a structure out of all my
books—what would wood

look like in that form?
Would the words stick
out facing the sky, or
would they be dripping
in, on my head, on my
everything. I don't know

how to save myself, any
how? most of the time?
I don't know mainly how
to save myself from my
words: I would want them
all, alive and well, or at
once, all at once, burning.

LOVE&POEM

To this day, we face the world
as one—the equation is simple
math: you and I: irregular irrep-
licable, but mostly irreplaceable.
There is no music to accompany
our exits—we'll proceed never
the less: the streets are one road:
the road is wide and open:
it's dark and clear—we know, we'
ve weaved together a way: begin
a beginning, though beginnings
are not for us, we look at each other:
we re-imagine and say: what's
being together mean anyway?
Together, we might be triangles:
pointy sharp corners going in and
out of bodies, drawing color
spilling blood. Boring or born
again? Did we cross the
in-between yet? Did we put a
number on that one, already?!
Any way, any where, we'll have
our steps: to run into each other
to cross one other, to walk in the
direction and against:
currents, trends, times—

Does this poem need the aid
       of a simile?

Let's try: like the veins
of a tree, we mark the years
without the finality of the
blade. On the surface, we look
apart but our roots must be touching.
Is there more room to say: I love you,
I miss you; I can't get you! Will I
Ever?
                Maybe…
the answer is no. At least it is, today.

PURE&LOVE

the object
doesn't
exist—

thus: no
one is
drawn

to another;
but what
if two

are drawn
together—
will this mean

you'll be wait-
ing for me in
the after-

life, where
figures
don't

have to touch?

benefit-cost-ratio
demands that the
canvas be as wide
as can be drawn

like an expansive
golf field confront-
ed by all the love
cliches: dawn, sun

etc. everywhere
every color is made
invisible by another
color; because the
heart can't pump love
all day, it takes it away
for matters of living—
isn't it sad to let go of

chance, for the sake
of the design, the
already given
        structure?

LIFE & DAWN

Both are drawn. This
is the blank falsity
of day. This: I take
as reality. Eyes can
or not. Look in or
out. There. Death
announcing itself
in squares, balanced
on the corner. Boxes,
like boxes that turn
out to be simple fact:
boxes, and more
boxes against
the sun, which I start
to draft, beginning
and brushing its light-
lock. Everywhere, the
mind is a god. Misstep
and you'll fall prey to
illusions. So: carry on
without starting. Be
the cause to be, because
one has to misstep in
order to defile, because
one has and one has not:

            etc.

SUMMER&SWEAT

You'll get used to it: this sweat.
It's sweet, you'll say: when it hits
your windowsill—you'll have to
stand still, to see it evaporate—
like the wind that has no body.
You, simply could keep still, and
elaborate on the kiss, which never
took place. Caution makes and
spoils every move, and what can
be done is all. Ready. Now mark
my words, sweet like salty sweat
and lovingly devoid of meaning—
Because I choose them carefully.
Only to please you. Though I can:
I choose not to guarantee a thing,
which, anyhow, has a mind of its
own. But look: these thoughts of
every passer-by who sees us in
love, could make us or break us:
so we sweat our fantasies falling
flat like dirt. Can anyone say what
is it? Does anyone get the gist…as
eyes lock to eyes, as breaths mingle
with air, as one drop of sweat hits
another, under your armpit. Could
this mass weigh you down towards
me, just one more bit? Could this coin

of sweat, forming your sweater, forming
a coinage between two bodies…could
it be a sign of luck, or is it just another
drop of sweat?

POET IN ANDALUSIA /
ANDALUSIA IN THE POET

◆

Sickness is the wait   for things
      to happen.

◆

Things don't care about happening:
They only appear in the light
and open their eyes
       to darkness—

Here   no tear
to shed
I only—
      escape language
to languid in another—
      hearing the
cries of the gypsies
      in Sevilla:
      then different eyes
cast their misery onto the river
of Arabic names:

why did I come to Andalusia?
to be stripped of it
      all.

So I can cry…like the gypsies
             who never found home.

    ♦

Here like everywhere, they can't leave
the tables and chairs alone—
             and like those sad songs
             of the gypsies

they have no one place.

They talk to the wind
all day
             and when they're grouped
             together

like a monstrous piece of
             modern art

             they don't complain
             much

because they know
they cannot be set
free

because they know
that sickness
is the wait.

◆

You can't tie the laces
of your shoes   in Alhambra:
water flows everywhere
to break the continuity of
any explanation: what's all this
                                    beauty?
Red stones make the heaven
and on the ground a piece of
it falls from a wall:
            I kick it, I pick it
            up—
I will hold it like a fallen
moon   in the corner
            of my pocket, where it
might sob silently
and burn itself out.

◆

Let's plaster our eyes
and give our lives
            to myth.

What a curse to be
blind   in Alhambra.

◆

The birds fly, and droppings
fall on beauty.

Nature doesn't care
for history.

History doesn't care
for anything.

They dance together
divided by a red veil

like a bull, and his
fighter in the ring:

our arrangements
for beauty grow

thin and thinner.

◆

O how weak is the simile
in a place that makes
constant demands
               on vision—

◆

The eyes grow cold.
Is it because the body
also grows old?
Or is it a malady?

This world of
       seeing
that renders the
       heart
an open void.

  ◆

On the way to Andalusia, the
train snakes through olive
groves or fields or farms—
the scene is so arranged
unlike the old olives of
       Palestine.

On the way to Catalonia
there are no olives, there
are lavender fields, also
so constructed, also an
industry where loot is
hiding in the blackest of
       eyes.

  ◆

The mirror offers me three
faces in Cordoba:
       who will I be
       today?

ANOTHER ONE FOR LORCA

◆

Granada is your name today!
Its hills come back, after their long absence, the one you
	dictated
by your own disappearance. Some call it your
	assassination—what an awful combination
of syllables.
But let's put words aside, and make a wall, so we can look
	over to those hills
because now they do
come back
to dance
with your shadow, yes,
the hills come back in their usual ups and downs.
Without the steps today, they move, and move some more;
	they bid us
more words, and move some
where, to that place we call
away.

◆

The hills again; they're singing their scenes:
They sigh their silent hymns; they shine their shallow
lands…and their empty broken roads
can only frown at all this light!
To them, the night is fair:
It hides their broken
bones.

◆

Alhambra is just an empty frame. It can't be real! It hangs above us
    all.
        In its halls, beauty screams:
I can't take it! I only want the fruit,
Granada, my Lorca! Everywhere you look,
its evenings fill the eye, and the Arabic tongue sticks out
like a lizard:

لا غالب إلا الله

◆

Your beloved gypsy songs are a thing
for the tourist now. All the wailing voices of the
 Granada nights sound so
Moorish. Is it really Arabic I hear in these recreations,
 or is nostalgia, our worst enemy
making a fool of me again?

◆

O sun…that sun…o sun: best
of the bullfighters. But the bull hides in shade, and these days,
these days without ends, without gore, approach us like
death. Every second we are closer to it. They approach without any
knowledge of what will be, and what will not. Is it, this death, as
        capable as
it used to be, as it was, when it made of us
prey. Is it still capable of making us bow and pray
at the alters of our own demise, moving us as close as can be
to the other side.

Don't tell me, Granada is a fortress for the picturesque world
that moves with its own people one more step towards beauty for
a selfie. I see them, moving moving to be captured
by their own devises, their created
selves—for the others to see, and only to see.

We roam the narrow roads of this city
and that—death hides its gore these days
and violence comes to us in calculated numbers
that are clear and clean, and we move on Lorca, to take
another image of ourselves.

THE AFTERLIVES OF
KETAMINE INFUSIONS

(point-zer0)

After mother's death, I had to face what my father didn't want
to: being alone with her absence. He married...etc. He did what's
best for him. And I went back to Philly, to stay on my own, alone,
with her disappearance. Where did she go? Is she only in that
grave, where the worms feast on her meek body, or is she some-
where else? The usual questions. Nothing new. I have no new
offerings—

For any

of you.

(poin1-one)

We cross out what's best for us—who are we? The walking
dead, the talking dead, running with the feet of those who gave
us life. What's it about, this merry-go-round. Again. No Answers.
Just a bunch of bricks, holding the edge of a door, in case it
    should slam,
and startle us in the middle of the night. Is it to see or to wheel
in ourselves a path, there for the tendency to be tense, and all
the way to curate the equation of life and death, that crumbles
into our minds as nonsense: only scarps that once in a while
    remind us of who we were; never who we are.

(point-2ow)

Water dumbs us down, and makes demands: we'll have to
wash the face with air, from now on…to keep alert, in dumb
ways, between sleep and death, comes a dreary dream, in
Arabic (the snaky script could sneak up on you, so beware!). Dogs
bark, and crickets don't do much around here, in this neck
of the woods, the U>S>A: only mad black figures roam the
streets and the corridors of this sad exchange, and when the
well-intentioned whites, give them a dollar or two, they feel so
and so. Did I give too much? Was I too good today? They will
come back and I'll have to turn them down one day, and mostly
everyday. It's ok, it's ok. I'll recycle my morals today, and buy
and buy some more, and put what I don't need on the side of
the road. For the figures to collect and add up. The well-off
can give no more. *It's potentially dangerous!* Those mothers-
and-fathers-and others. Let me say no more—who am I? I fa-
thom we are overloaded with intuition, and the world never
                              made sense anyway.

(point-t3ree)

After ketamine, I kept calling for my mother: yamma yamma!
Can you show me a face of yours? I remember the last one so
well, and I want you to show me a face in your youth that I've
never seen. I say to myself: ketamine and the dream, keta-
Kate, the name of that nurse: please dear sustenance show
me that pure green, where I would step into the afterlife for
a moment with my mother. I close my eyes to see pure color

I plant the dead in this city or that. I keep moving in circles off
course. My usual trick is to plant dead things under dirt. I, no.
So I call again for you: yamma yamma yamma, and the call
falls short, it misses the mark (as always?). And for what?
This babble can't fill the mouth like shrubs and other healthy
plants do. Dill is one example I hate to chew. I've never been
much of a gardener. But I try to plant dead trees in the city garden
offered to me by the gods. I do that for Christmas trees, while
all the neighbors drag theirs to the side of the road, or the good
ones drag them to the farmers market, to be turned to dust. So
this is what's it coming down to...the old ways! So yes, please,
       let's deal the world another blow—

(point-4our)

Stealth is the first step into progress. My hands take away what's
mine. That's no good. You must reach for the things of others.
       Even
better, for the lands of others. Progress. It's supposed to be good
for you, for you, and only you. I want to try this, and after my
       ketamine
infusion I reach for another bottle of water that was not offered to
me. I also reach for one of the sleeping blinds, to take home. How
much is it? I puff up the figure as a true capitalist—this is
       $3000: now
stealing a touch is another story. I gather touch is a hard thing
       to steal.
What about the words we sneak behind an act—to justify murder,
among other trivial things. So I steal my drink, I put the blind
       in my

pocket. And after ketamine I steal a glass of wine I'm not supposed
to have—only to complete a coaster poem in a dirty bar. Then
    I go,
that same night to fuck up my mind even more. I go to the
    woodshop—
I feel like giving back…maybe my fingers to the table saw. Wood
shouldn't be the only thing fed to the blade, bones could also
    splinter
at the teeth of a saw. Bones could be the new wood, and red, well, is
            as old and boring as our failings.

(point-infinit&)

Where my lies have caught up with my reasoning, is where I draw
the line. What else can I draw. Someone tells me: *you don't look
any better than that*! I want to say, there is something off with your
phrasing, but instead I take it as it is, and straight to heart, where
hurt burns my ribs, and infects my vital organs, only to
    sustain some
fire in me, as I put my anger on neutral. Maybe a hint of the living
is what I need. Not calling for the dead during my treatment. But
I feel differently. Only a hint of living that connects me with
    the dead
is what I need. So I go back—to that back I don't believe in
    anymore
and you ask me: where…where…where…and I tell you that I'll let

                    You

                              know

        when I'm there.

A LAMENT

for Zbigniew Herbert

And then notes. No more poems: I've read everything,
every line, god damn it! Did I learn anything from you?
Maybe too much, maybe nothing, I don't think you meant
to give lessons, although you did: but to no-one, no
one in particular…you wanted the world to learn some
thing, yes an object, and stick with it, leaving each other
be. How level the mind can be. Etc. before anything.
How cynicism sinks like lead, how heavy!

We have no way of holding onto the shapes
we like. We are bored. Our record of clouds is diminishing
into more clouds. Beside all the things stuck in my mind,
how I wish I can keep you, your words and arrangements,
       but things get pushed
out. And hopelessly, you and I can't keep
       together
           or apart.

ACKNOWLEDGMENTS & NOTES

Many thanks to the editors and journals where versions of the following poems appeared:

"Lose Strings" in *Massachusetts Review*

"Before Gaza, A Fall" in *Prairie Schooner*

"Holy Land, Wasted" and "Wrong Winds" in *LitHub,* and I'm including here my note that accompanied my collaboration with Huda Fakhreddine on the former poem:

I began writing this poem on my way to Palestine on December 25th, 2023. I sent early sections to Huda as I was writing and her comments started taking the form of stanzas, so I invited her to write more. We were writing to each other, back and forth; I, in Bethlehem, and she, in Philadelphia, with nothing on our minds but Gaza.

We each have a relationship with T.S. Eliot's poem and found writing against it, and through it, a way of centering the horrors of this unprecedented moment. The idea was to displace 'The Waste Land,' to challenge its Eurocentric currents and place it in Gaza now, and in Palestine in general. A 'wasteland' is being created in 'the holy land,' and has been for the past 75 years. As always, the American-European war machine is mobilized to wreak terror in the lands of 'others.'

The world is complicit in the horrors we are witnessing in Gaza and in Palestine today. Time from now on will be marked by Gaza, and its movement only toward a free Palestine.

"Some Verses for the Depressed Rebel" in Poem-a-Day of the *Academy of American Poets*. In this poem the first line "Fame is a B." echoes the line by Emily Dickinson "Fame is a bee" but it might as well be "fame is a bitch."

"Pure&Love" in *Jewish Currents*

My utmost gratitude to Adie B. Steckel who was gracious enough to recommend my previous book to readers and to help me prepare and offer this one to them.

FONO
GRAꟻ

1. **Eileen Myles**—*Aloha/irish trees* (LP)

2. **Rae Armantrout**—*Conflation* (LP)

3. **Alice Notley**—*Live in Seattle* (LP)

4. **Harmony Holiday**—*The Black Saint and the Sinnerman* (LP)

5. **Susan Howe & Nathaniel Mackey**—*STRAY: A Graphic Tone* (LP)

6. **Annelyse Gelman & Jason Grier**—*About Repulsion* (EP)

7. **Joshua Beckman**—*Some Mechanical Poems To Be Read Aloud* (print)

8. **Dao Strom**—*Instrument/ Traveler's Ode* (print; cassette tape)

9. **Douglas Kearney & Val Jeanty**—*Fodder* (LP)

10. **Mark Leidner**—*Returning the Sword to the Stone* (print)

11. **Charles Valle**—*Proof of Stake: An Elegy* (print)

12. **Emily Kendal Frey**—*LOVABILITY* (print)

13. **Brian Laidlaw and the Family Trade**—*THIS ASTER: adaptations of Emile Nelligan* (LP)

14. **Nathaniel Mackey and The Creaking Breeze Ensemble**—*Fugitive Equation* (compact disc)

15. *FE Magazine* (print)

16. **Brandi Katherine Herrera**—*MOTHER IS A BODY* (print)

17. **Jan Verberkmoes**—*Firewatch* (print)

18. **Krystal Languell**—*Systems Thinking with Flowers* (print)

19. **Matvei Yankelevich**—*Dead Winter* (print)

20. **Cody-Rose Clevidence**—*Dearth & God's Green Mirth* (print)

Fonograf Editions is a registered 501(c)(3) nonprofit organization. Find more information about the press at: fonografeditions.com.